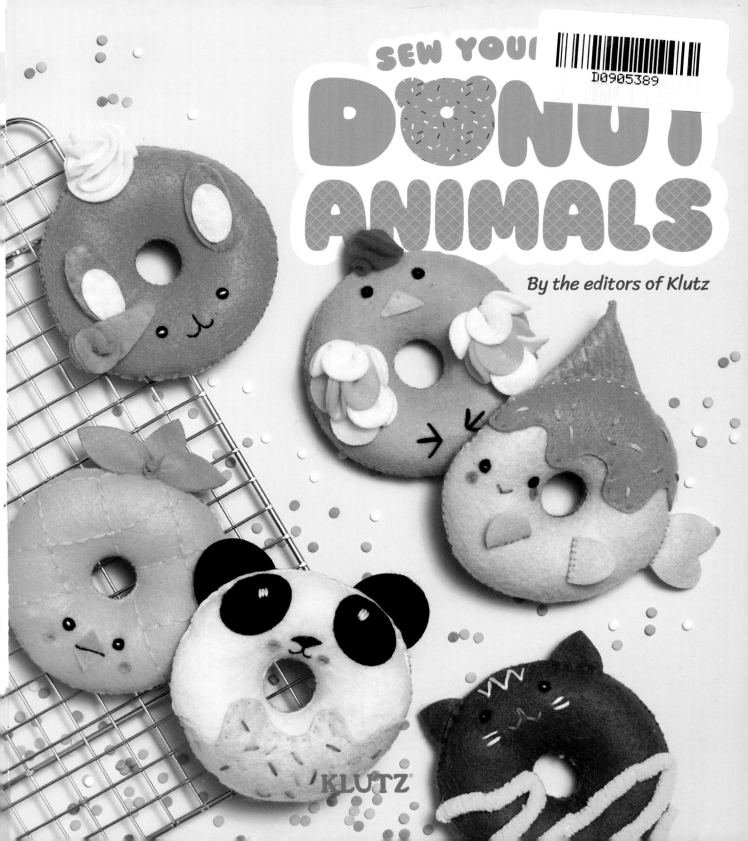

SEW YOUR DONUT ANIMALS

By the editors of Klutz

KLUTZ

D0905389

KLUTZ® creates activity books and other great stuff for kids ages 3 to 103. We began our corporate life in 1977 in a garage we shared with a Chevrolet Impala. Although we've outgrown that first office, Klutz galactic headquarters is still staffed entirely by real human beings. For those of you who collect mission statements, here's ours:

CREATE WONDERFUL THINGS • BE GOOD • HAVE FUN

Paper sourced from Brazil and Finland. All other parts assembled and made in China. 156

©2020 Klutz. All rights reserved.

Published by Klutz, a subsidiary of Scholastic Inc. Scholastic and associated logos are trademarks and/or registered trademarks of Scholastic Inc. Klutz and associated logos are trademarks and/or registered trademarks of Klutz. The "book and box" format is a registered trademark of Klutz. No part of this publication may be reproduced in any form or by any means without written permission of Klutz. For information regarding permission, please contact Klutz, Attn: Permissions Department, 557 Broadway, New York, NY 10012.

Distributed in the UK by
Scholastic UK Ltd
Euston House
24 Eversholt Street
London, NW1 1DB
United Kingdom

Distributed in Canada by
Scholastic Canada Ltd
604 King Street West
Toronto, Ontario
Canada M5V 1E1

Distributed in Australia by
Scholastic Australia Ltd
PO Box 579
Gosford, NSW
Australia 2250

Distributed in Hong Kong by
Scholastic Hong Kong Ltd
Suites 2001-2, Top Glory Tower
262 Gloucester Road
Causeway Bay, Hong Kong

WRITE US

We would love to hear your comments regarding this or any of our books.

KLUTZ®
557 Broadway
New York, NY 10012
thefolks@klutz.com

FSC
www.fsc.org
MIX
Paper from responsible sources
FSC® C119793

This product is made of FSC®-certified and other controlled material. FSC® is dedicated to the promotion of responsible forest management world-wide.

ISBN 978-1-338-56615-4
4 1 5 8 5 7 0 8 8 8

BOX: Photo ©: donut: A_Ple/Shutterstock. CASE: Photo ©: inside pattern: Anastasiia_2305/Shutterstock.

CONTENTS

START HERE!

DELICIOUS DONUTS

Donut start the party without us!

WHAT YOU GET

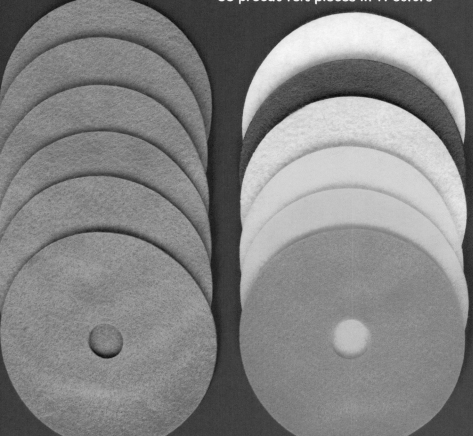

66 precut felt pieces in 11 colors

Precut felt eyes

Precut felt cheeks

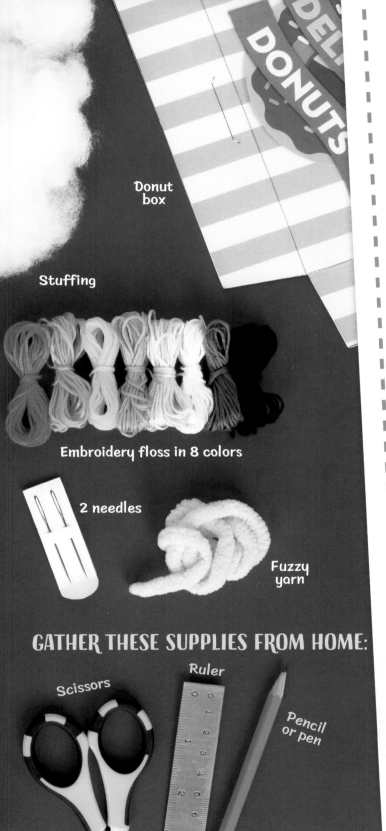

Donut box

Stuffing

Embroidery floss in 8 colors

2 needles

Fuzzy yarn

GATHER THESE SUPPLIES FROM HOME:

Scissors

Ruler

Pencil or pen

SAFETY STUFF

» Always handle needles with care. Don't rush the stitches.

» Needles are sharp. If you have a thimble, wear it to protect your fingertips while stitching.

» Keep needles away from small children, pets, and bare feet.

» Store your needles when you're finished working. You can use the needle holder provided or a pin cushion of your choice.

» If a needle breaks, carefully check the surrounding area and throw out broken needle pieces.

» If a needle breaks the skin, gently clean the area and apply a bandage. Get an adult to help you.

» These donuts and accessories are for decoration only. Do not give them to small children to play with.

» If the project gets dirty, spot-clean only with a damp rag and warm water. Do not wash the donuts in a washing machine.

» Store loose strands of floss and other craft supplies away from pets and babies.

» Use supplies included only for projects in this kit.

Using Floss

The embroidery floss in this book has six thin strands twisted together. To make decorations like sprinkles, you can use floss straight from the bundle. Otherwise, you'll use two strands at a time. Here's how you separate the strands.

1 Unwind the bundle of embroidery floss. Cut a strand of floss about 14 inches (35.5 cm) long.

2 Hold the floss gently in one hand, about 1 inch (2.5 cm) from the end.

3 With your other hand, pull one strand of floss up...

Always separate the threads one at a time.

...and away from the rest of the bundle.

4 You now have one strand of floss. Repeat Steps 2–3 so you have two strands total.

5 Line up the two strands so the ends meet up. Smooth them down. You're all set to sew!

Keep extra strands of floss loose and untangled, so you can use them later.

THREADING THE NEEDLE

You can tie a few knots in the same place to make a chunkier knot.

1 Tie a knot in one end of your floss. Loop the end across the main part of the strand . . .

. . . then lead the end under the main floss and through the loop . . .

. . . and finally pull the end to tighten the knot.

2 Moisten the other end of the floss. Pinch the end to help make it pointy.

3 Hold the needle in one hand, and push the pointy end of the thread through the loop, or "eye," of the needle.

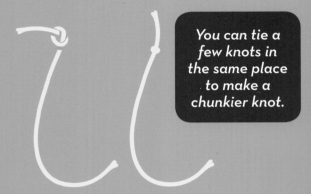

4 Your needle is now threaded! There are two tails of floss. The long end with the knot will sew in and out of the fabric. The short end should hang about 4 inches (10 cm) past the needle to help keep the floss in place.

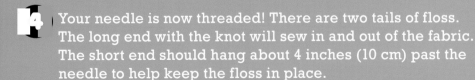

COOKIES & CREAM PANDA

Start here! Make this sprinkled-with-love bear first to become a master donut maker. Get ready . . . it's going to be *PANDA*licious!

BLACK, WHITE, & SPRINKLES ALL OVER!

Sew Sprinkles

1 Thread your needle with your first color of floss (page 7).

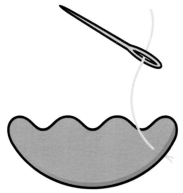

YOU WILL NEED

- ☐ Blue icing
- ☐ Needle
- ☐ Floss in yellow, pink, white, and green
- ☐ Scissors

2 Poke the needle up through the back of the felt. Pull gently until the knot touches the back of the felt.

3 Poke your needle back down through the felt, ¼ inch (6 mm) from where you poked it up. Check it out! You just made your first stitch.

4 Repeat Steps 2–3 to make another stitch about 1 inch (2.5 cm) away from your first stitch. Sprinkles look random, so make your stitches at wonky angles.

5 Keep making stitches all over the felt until you have 6 stitches in your first color.

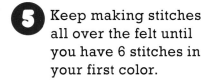

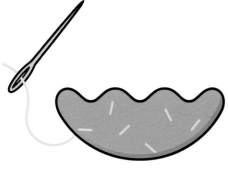

Your stitch is on the front, or "right" side of the felt. Your knot is on the back of the felt, which is called the "wrong" side. The wrong side won't be visible when you're finished, so it's OK if it looks a little messy.

9

FINISH YOUR FLOSS WITH AN ENDING KNOT

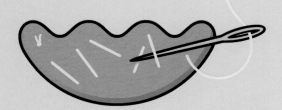

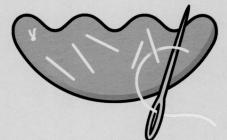

6 Turn your felt over so the back (wrong side) is facing you. Poke your needle under one of the nearby stitches (but don't poke the felt!) to make a loop.

7 Pass your needle through the loop, and pull to tighten.

8 Repeat Steps 6–7 for a super strong knot.

If your floss isn't long enough, or you're having trouble, don't fret!

- *Remove the needle from the floss.*
- *Separate the floss into two strands.*
- *Tie a knot with the two strands.*

9 Trim the thread's tail with scissors if it's long.

10 Repeat Steps 3–9 with the other sprinkle colors until you've made a rad rainbow topping.

NOW YOU'RE READY TO GET BAKING!

Add the Icing

YOU WILL NEED

☐ White donut front
☐ Blue icing
☐ Blue floss
☐ Scissors

STRAIGHT STITCH

1 Stack the icing on top of the white felt (right sides facing up) so the curved edges line up.

Your topping has two sides: a curved side and a squiggly side.

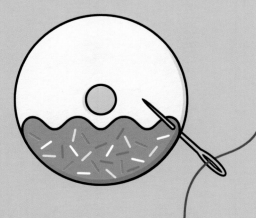

2 Start at the corner, where the curved side and the squiggly side meet. Thread your needle with two strands of blue floss (page 7) and poke it up through the white felt and the blue felt.

3 Pull your floss so that the knot is against the back of the white felt.

4 Make a stitch, poking your needle down through both pieces of felt.

5 Poke your needle back up through both pieces of felt.

6 Keep making stitches this way all along the squiggly edge of the felt.

7 Stop when you get to the end of the squiggly side. You won't need to stitch the curved side right now. Finish your floss (page 10).

The stitches will look like little dashes, with gaps between each stitch. This is called a "straight stitch."

Make the Face

YOU WILL NEED

- Panda-in-progress
- Panda eye patches x 2
- Panda nose
- Floss in black, white, and pink
- Felt cheeks x 2
- Scissors

1 The icing is on the bottom half of the donut. Place the panda eye patches on the top half.

2 Thread your needle with black floss (page 7). Straight stitch around the edge of one eye patch to attach it to the panda body. Finish your floss (page 10).

3 Repeat Step 2 with the other eye.

4 Thread your needle with all six strands of white floss. Make a small stitch through the right panda eye so the floss is toward one end of the oval.

5 Make three more stitches right alongside your first stitch, so you've made a little patch of white that pops against the dark eye patch.

6 Repeat Steps 4–5 with the left eye.

7 Thread your needle with pink floss to attach the cheeks with one stitch, ½ inch (13 mm) below eyes.

8 Use black floss to attach the panda nose between the eyes with two stitches. Make sure to finish your floss (page 10).

MAKE THE MOUTH

BACK STITCH

1 Use black floss to make a stitch just under the nose, slanted a little left.

2 Now poke the needle up one stitch-length away from your first stitch, a little farther down and to the left.

3 To make your second stitch, poke your needle into the same spot where you finished your first stitch.

4 Keep back stitching a tiny curve to the left, and then repeat Steps 1–3 to stitch a tiny curve to the right. Now you've got a bear-y cute smile! Don't forget to finish your floss (page 10).

See how you made a stitch by looping back to where you started? That's why this is called a back stitch! You can use back stitches to make lines with no gaps. Great for grins and other details!

Sew the Donut Hole

WHIP STITCH

1 Stack the donut front on the donut back, with the right side facing up.

2 With a needle threaded with white floss, poke up through just the front layer, ¼ inch (6 mm) away from the center hole. Pull the floss so the knot is against the inside of the front layer.

3 Now loop the needle around and poke up through the back and front layers, close to your first stitch. Pull the needle through to make one whip stitch.

4 Whip stitch along the edge of the center hole. When you get back to where you started, finish your floss between the layers of the donut, so it's hidden (page 10).

TOTAL HOLE IN ONE!

STUFFING & FINISHING

1 Sandwich the flat edge of the ears between front and back layers.

2 With a needle threaded with white floss, begin to whip stitch the outer edges of the front and back together (page 16).

3 When you get to an ear, use a straight stitch (page 11) to sew all the layers together. After you finish the ear, return to whip stitching. Stop stitching when you are 2 inches (5 cm) away from where you started stitching, so there is a gap.

If you run out of floss while you're stitching, no problem! Just finish your floss where you are, and start stitching from there with new floss.

4 Add pinches of stuffing until your donut is nice and puffy. Then whip stitch the gap closed and finish your floss (page 10).

THE SWEET SQUAD

WAFFLE CONE NARWHAL

OUR WAFFLE CONES ARE ALSO PARTY HATS!

Donuts + ice cream = SEAriously sweet!

YOU WILL NEED

- ☐ *Blue donut front*
- ☐ *Eyes x 2*
- ☐ *Cheeks x 2*
- ☐ *Floss in pink, white, and blue*
- ☐ *Pink icing*
- ☐ *Needle*
- ☐ *Scissors*
- ☐ *Fins x 2*
- ☐ *Tail*
- ☐ *Donut back*
- ☐ *Stuffing*
- ☐ *Horn*

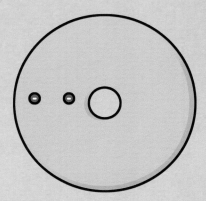

1 Place the eyes on the left side of the blue felt, about ½ inch (13 mm) from the edge. Use a needle threaded with white floss to stitch them to the felt.

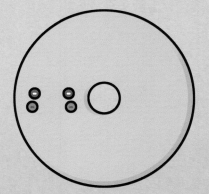

2 Use pink floss to stitch the cheeks to the felt under the eyes.

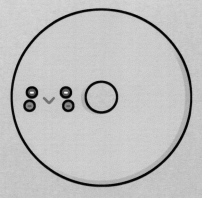

3 Use back stitch to make a little **V** shape with pink floss between the cheeks for a sweet smile.

4 Lay the fins below the face and whip stitch (page 16) their straight edges to the front of the donut. Finish your floss (page 10).

5 Line up the curved edge of the icing with the top of the donut. Use pink floss to straight stitch (page 11) the squiggly edge of the icing to the donut. Hold off on stitching the curved edge for now.

STUFFING & FINISHING

6 Your horn has two straight edges and one curved edge. Line up the straight edges and whip stitch them together with pink floss. Finish your floss (page 10).

7 Sandwich the curved edge of the horn and the straight edge of the tail between the donut layers. The horn goes at the top, and the tail goes on the right side.

8 Using a needle threaded with blue floss, follow the instructions on pages 16–17 to stitch and stuff your donut.

COCO KITTY
COSMICALLY CUTE CATS!
CHOCOLATE RINGS WITH MILKY WAY ICING!

YOU WILL NEED

- Needle
- Chocolate donut front
- Eyes x 2
- Floss in white, pink, and brown
- White fuzzy yarn
- Ears x 2
- Donut back
- Stuffing
- Scissors

1 Place the eyes ½ inch (13 mm) away from the outer edge of the donut front. They should be 1 inch (2.5 cm) away from each other. Stitch them to the front with white floss. They will be the top of your donut.

2 Back stitch two little **U** shapes between the eyes in pink floss to make the kitty mouth.

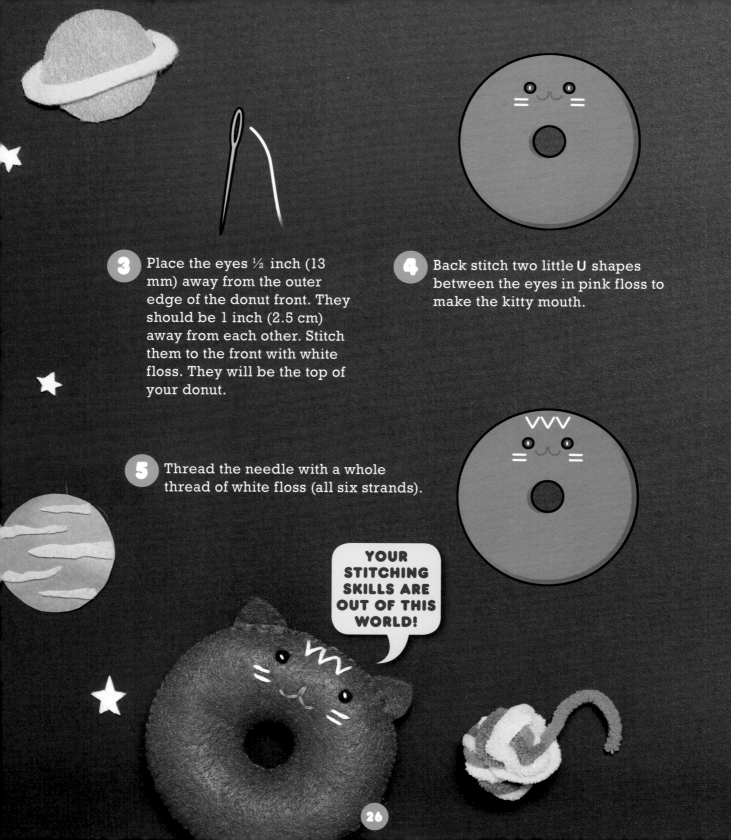

3 Place the eyes ½ inch (13 mm) away from the outer edge of the donut front. They should be 1 inch (2.5 cm) away from each other. Stitch them to the front with white floss. They will be the top of your donut.

4 Back stitch two little **U** shapes between the eyes in pink floss to make the kitty mouth.

5 Thread the needle with a whole thread of white floss (all six strands).

YOUR STITCHING SKILLS ARE OUT OF THIS WORLD!

Drizzle

Fluffy yarn gives your donut fancy frosting!

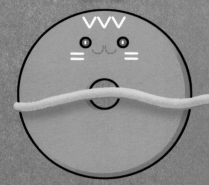

6 You will attach the fluffy yarn to the donut later, but first it helps to map out where it will go. Lay your fluffy yarn over your donut front, with one end at the outer edge on the left side of the donut.

7 Zigzag the yarn across the donut a few times to make a delightful drizzle!

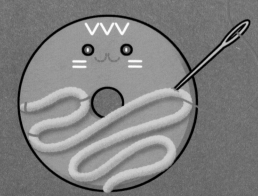

8 With a needle threaded with pink floss, make a stitch over the yarn and through the felt to hold the yarn in place. Finish your floss (page 10). Repeat this at every zigzag corner.

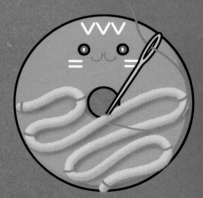

9 Make stitches to attach the yarn where it crosses the middle line of the donut (below the inner hole).

10 Repeat pages 16–17 to assemble your cool coco kitty!

YOU WILL NEED

- [ ] Needle
- [ ] Yellow donut front
- [ ] Eyes x 2
- [ ] Floss in white, pink, and yellow
- [ ] Cheeks x 2
- [ ] Ruler
- [ ] Pointy leaves x 3
- [ ] Donut back
- [ ] Stuffing
- [ ] Pencil or fine-tipped pen

Make the Face

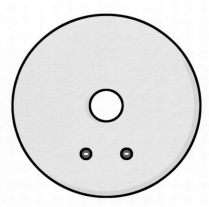

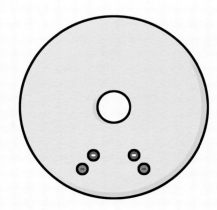

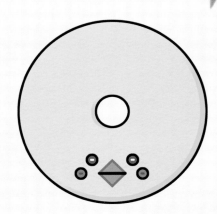

1 Using white floss, stitch the eyes to the donut front ½ inch (13 mm) away from the outer edge, and 1 inch (2.5 cm) apart from one another. This face will be the bottom of the donut.

2 With pink floss, stitch one cheek to the donut front, halfway between the right eye and the edge. It will be about ¼ inch (6 mm) away from the eye. Do the same with the other cheek below the left eye.

3 Place the beak between the cheeks so the sharper ends are pointing up and down (like a diamond). Thread your needle with black floss and use back stitch to sew the beak to the face.

29

Plan Your Pattern

4 The pineapple pattern is a grid. It's easy to stitch once you map where the stitches will go. Start by using a ruler and lining it up across the **wrong side** of the donut front at a slant. You don't want to stitch over the face, so make sure the ruler doesn't cross the face.

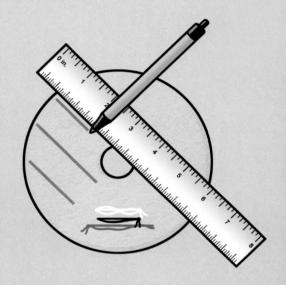

5 With a pencil or pen, make slanted lines in one direction.

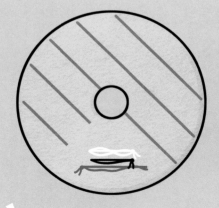

6 Draw slanted lines in the opposite direction.

7 Flip your felt over to the right side. With a whole thread (all 6 strands) of yellow floss, back stitch the grid on the right side. You'll use the lines you drew on the wrong side to guide where your needle will poke up. Keep flipping back and forth to make sure your stitching is straight.

This part uses some serious stitching power! It's OK to take a break if you need to before you start again.

MAKE A CLUSTER OF LEAVES

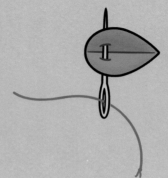

8 Fold one leaf long ways like a hot dog bun. With a needle threaded with green floss, poke through one end of the leaf, close to the pointy tip. Make sure your needle goes through both layers of the fold. Pull your needle through so the knot is against the leaf.

9 Without finishing your floss, repeat Step 8 so your thread has two leaves strung like beads. Repeat again with the third leaf.

10 Pull the thread tight so the leaves bunch up at one end. Tie a knot but don't snip your floss!

11 Attach your leaves to the top of the donut front with a few stitches. Finish your floss (page 10).

12 Repeat Step 8 with yellow floss to make each wing. Attach the wings on either side of the face with a few stitches. Then, follow pages 16–17 to put your donut together.

WHAT'S-ITS-FACE

Use your stitching skills to give your donuts different moods and attitudes.

SLEEPY EYES

WINKY EYES

HAPPY EYES

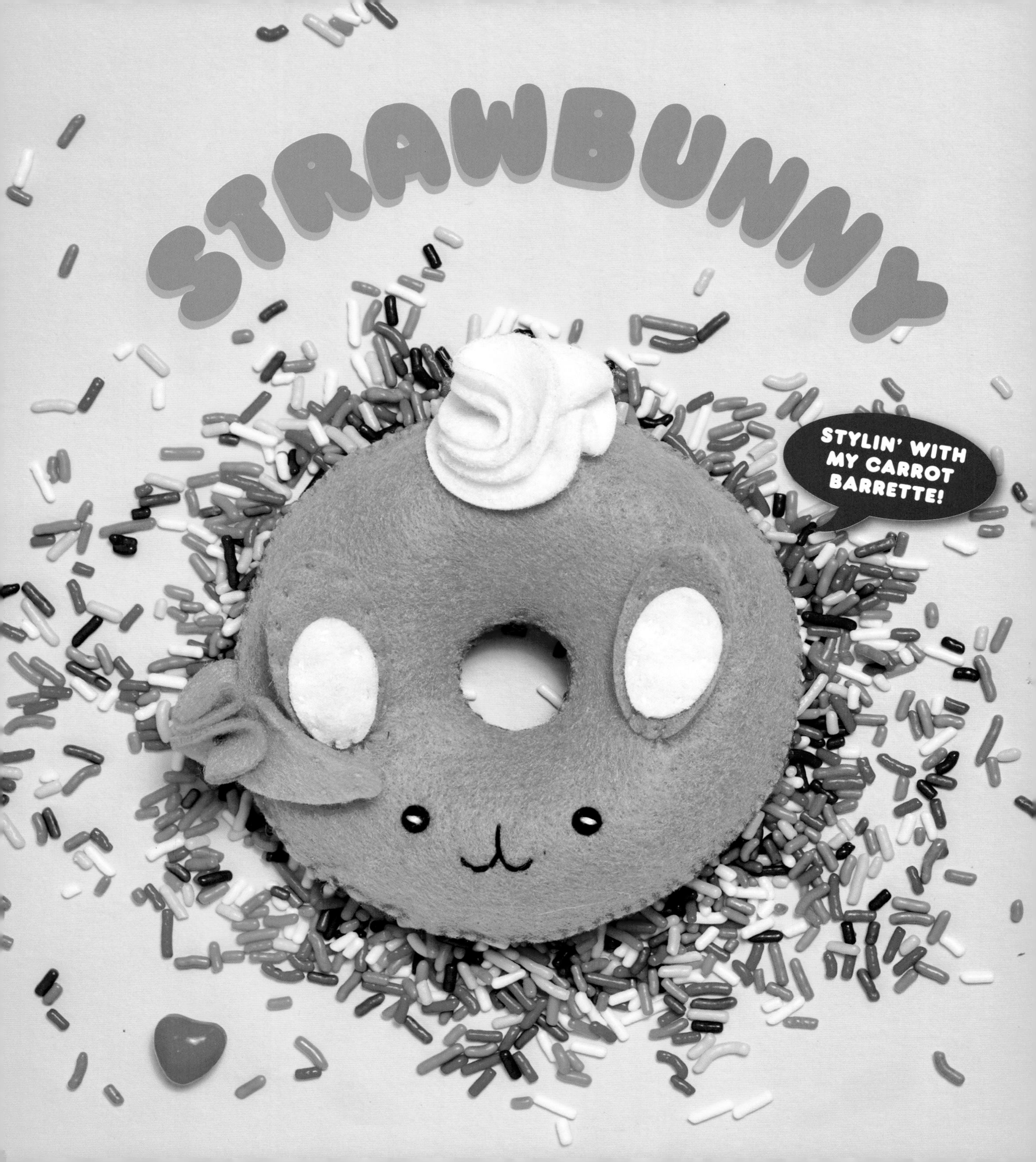
STRAWBUNNY
STYLIN' WITH MY CARROT BARRETTE!

- ☐ *Pink donut front*
- ☐ *Eyes x 2*
- ☐ *Floss in white, black, pink, green, and orange*
- ☐ *Cheeks x 2*
- ☐ *White oval x 2*
- ☐ *Pink oval x 2*
- ☐ *Large white circles x 5*
- ☐ *Carrot x 2*
- ☐ *Green circles x 3*

1 Using white floss, stitch the eyes to the donut front ½ inch (13 mm) away from the outer edge, and 1 inch (2.5 cm) apart from one another. This face will be toward the bottom of the donut.

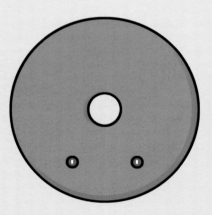

2 Thread the needle with black floss and use back stitch to make a little **w** shape between the eyes for the bunny mouth.

3 Stack an inner ear on top of an outer ear. With a needle threaded with white floss, use a straight stitch around the edge of the inner ear. Stack this layer on top of another pink outer ear and straight stitch the outer ears together with pink floss. Finish your floss (page 10) and repeat with the other inner and outer ear.

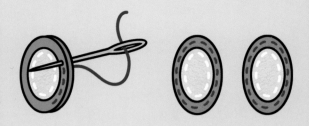

4 Place the ears above the face on either side of the donut hole. Thread the needle with pink floss and straight stitch around the edge of one ear to attach it to the donut front. Do the same with the other ear.

SURE WISH THIS WAS A DONUT!

MAKE A TUFT

The bunny tail is made of three felt circles that are grouped into a tuft.

1 To make the first tuft, fold three circles in half, making three tacos.

2 Thread your needle with white floss and poke it through the middle of the folded edge of one taco. Do the same with the other tacos.

You can fold and move the layers of the tuft around to get a nice fluffy shape.

3 Pull the thread tight so the tacos bunch up in a tuft and make an ending knot, but don't snip your floss!

4 With the folded side facing down (touching the donut felt) whip stitch the tuft to the donut felt at the top of the donut.

MAKE THE CARROT

1 Use orange floss to straight stitch the carrot layers together.

2 Follow the instructions on page 37 (Steps 1–4) to make a tuft with the green circles and attach them to the top of the carrot.

3 Sew the carrot onto the strawbunny with a few stitches.

4 Repeat pages 16–17 to assemble your strawbunny!

YOU WILL NEED

- ☐ Orange donut front
- ☐ Eyes x 2
- ☐ Floss in white, black, and orange
- ☐ Yellow triangle
- ☐ Red circles x 9
- ☐ Yellow circles x 6
- ☐ White circles x 12
- ☐ Donut back

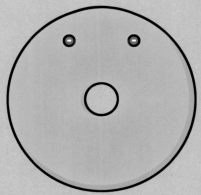

1 Place the eyes ½ inch (13 mm) away from the outer edge of the donut front. They should be 1 inch (2.5 cm) away from each other. Stitch them to the front with white floss. They will be the top of your donut.

2 Line up the tip of the yellow triangle between the eyes, pointing up. Thread your needle with yellow floss and use a straight stitch along the edge of the triangle to sew it to the donut front.

3 Thread a needle with orange floss. To make the chicken's comb, Repeat Steps 1–4 (page 37) using red circles. Attach them to the top of the donut front above the eyes.

4 Thread your needle with a whole strand (all 6 threads) of black floss, and get ready to make some really neat chicken feet.

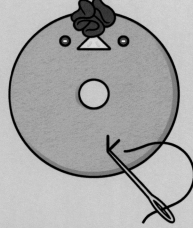

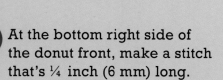

5 At the bottom right side of the donut front, make a stitch that's ¼ inch (6 mm) long.

6 Use back stitch to make two stitches on either side of the first. Poke your needle down through the same spot as your first stitch. This will make an arrow shape that points down.

7 Repeat Steps 5–6 on the bottom left side of the donut front.

WHIP UP SOME WINGS

*Each of the wings is made of 9 felt circles,
grouped into three clusters of feathers.*

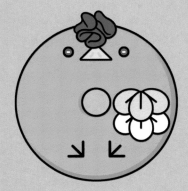

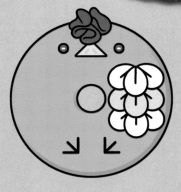

1 Follow the instructions (page 32, Steps 8–11) to make a cluster of three white feathers. Then sew them to one side of the donut front.

2 Repeat Step 1 to add a layer of three yellow feathers over the white feathers . . .

. . . then a layer of white feathers on top.

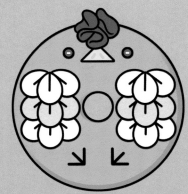

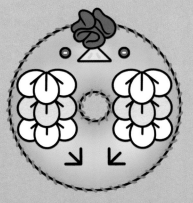

3 Repeat Steps 1–2 on the other side of the donut front.

4 Your chicken's almost ready to fly the coop! Repeat the steps on pages 16–17 to put together and stuff the donut.

PUT TOGETHER YOUR BAKER'S BOX

Donut start the party without us!

1 You can find the donut box inside the kit! Fold the box along the score lines with the white sides facing in, starting with the square tabs.

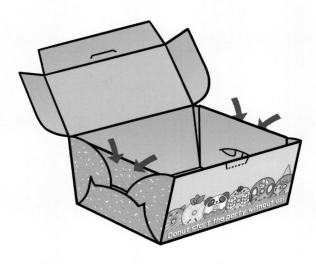

2 There are little tabs on the sides decorated with sprinkles. Tuck these tabs into the side slot.

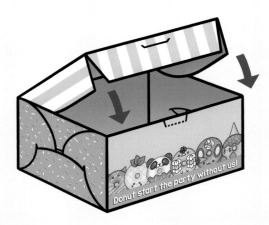

3 Tuck the tabs decorated with stripes into the inside of the box.

4 The front of the box has a tiny blue tab in the middle. To keep the top secure, fold this tab behind the striped tab.

HANGIN' AROUND

Fold a ribbon in half and stitch the ends of the ribbon to the back of the donut.

DONUT DÉCOR

Here are some out-of-the box ideas for displaying your cute creations!

SWEET FEET

Now that you know your stitches, sew a pair of donuts to the top of slippers. Comfy and cute!

SPRINKLE STYLE

A thermos sleeve is a perfect donut accessory you can stitch up using felt from your local craft store.

CREDITS

DOUGH PROOFER: Maria Rogers

SUGAR ARTIST: Vanessa Han

TECHNICAL ILLUSTRATOR: Kyle Hilton

GLAZER: Owen Keating

BAKER'S DOZEN BUYER: Roxy Leung

PHOTOGRAPHER: Lucy Schaeffer

SPRINKLE TECHNICIAN: Gina Kim

TASTE TESTER: Sam Walker

BUNNY BAKER: Marley Rhoma Miranda

SPECIAL THANKS TO: Caitlin Harpin, Stacy Lellos, Netta Rabin, and Heidi Hankaniemi

Get creative with more from KLUTZ

Looking for more goof-proof activities, sneak peeks, and giveaways? Find us online!

KlutzCertified KlutzCertified KlutzCertified KlutzCertified Klutz

Klutz.com • thefolks@klutz.com • 1-800-737-4123